**BOA**
EDITIONS LTD

*Refuge*

D1307309

# Refuge

*Poems by*
ADRIE KUSSEROW

AMERICAN POETS CONTINUUM SERIES, No. 137

BOA EDITIONS, LTD. ❧ ROCHESTER, NY ❧ 2013

Copyright © 2013 by Adrie Kusserow
All rights reserved
Manufactured in the United States of America

First Edition
13 14 15 16 7 6 5 4 3 2 1

For information about permission to reuse any material from this book please contact The Permissions Company at www.permissionscompany.com or e-mail permdude@eclipse.net.

Publications by BOA Editions, Ltd.—a not-for-profit corporation under section 501 (c) (3) of the United States Internal Revenue Code—are made possible with funds from a variety of sources, including public funds from the New York State Council on the Arts, a state agency; the Literature Program of the National Endowment for the Arts; the County of Monroe, NY; the Lannan Foundation for support of the Lannan Translations Selection Series; the Mary S. Mulligan Charitable Trust; the Rochester Area Community Foundation; the Arts & Cultural Council for Greater Rochester; the Steeple-Jack Fund; the Ames-Amzalak Memorial Trust in memory of Henry Ames, Semon Amzalak and Dan Amzalak; and contributions from many individuals nationwide. See Colophon on page 82 for special individual acknowledgments.

**ART WORKS.**
arts.gov

State of the Arts

NYSCA

Cover Design: Sandy Knight
Cover Art: Pete Muller
Interior Design and Composition: Richard Foerster
Manufacturing: McNaughton & Gunn
BOA Logo: Mirko

Library of Congress Cataloging-in-Publication Data

Kusserow, Adrie.
  [Poems]
  Refuge : poems / by Adrie Kusserow. — First edition.
      pages cm
  Poems.
  ISBN 978-1-938160-08-0 (pbk.) — ISBN 978-1-938160-09-7 (Ebook)
  I. Title.
  PS3611.U74R44 2013
  811'.6—dc23
                          2012044340

BOA Editions, Ltd.
250 North Goodman Street, Suite 306
Rochester, NY 14607
www.boaeditions.org
*A. Poulin, Jr., Founder (1938–1996)*

*For my family
and for all refugees everywhere.*

The Lost Boys (and Girls) refers to 20,000 children in southern Sudan that fled their homes seeking refuge from the second Sudanese civil war. They walked 1,000 miles before they finally found protection in refugee camps in Ethiopia and Kenya. Half of them died along the way. About 3,800 have been resettled in America. There is currently a second wave of Lost Boys and Girls now fleeing the bombings in the Nuba Mountains of Sudan.

# Contents

We now have access, increasingly, to more and more cultures across the globe, and the result is that restlessness has gone global. . . . the sense of an answer to be found somewhere else.

—Pico Iyer, *The Open Road: The Global Journey of the Fourteenth Dalai Lama*

## Skull Trees, South Sudan

For Atem Deng

Arok Deng, hiding from the Arabs in the branches of a tree,
two weeks surviving on leaves,
legs numb, mouth dry.
When the mosquitoes swarmed
and the bodies settled limp as petals under the trees,
he shinnied down, scooping out a mud pit with his hands
sliding into it like a snake,
his whole body covered except his mouth.
Perhaps others were near him,
lying in gloves of mud, sucking bits of air through the swamp holes,
mosquitoes biting their lips,
but he dared not look.

What did he know of the rest of South Sudan, pockmarked with bombs,
skull trees with their necklaces of bones,
packs of bony Lost Boys
roving like hyenas toward Ethiopia,
tongues, big as toads, swelling in their mouths,

the sky pouring its relentless bombs of fire. Of course they were
tempted to lie down for a moment,

under the lone tree, with its barely shade,
to rest just a little while before moving on,

the days passing slyly, hallucinations
floating like kites above them

until the blanched bones lay scattered in a ring around the tree,
tiny ribs, skulls, hip bones—a tea set overturned,
as the hot winds whistled through them
as they would anything, really,

and the sky, finally exhausted,
moving on.

## The Unraveling Strangeness

You are losing it, they say,
        paranoid delusions of soldiers breaking into your house,

hiding your car from the police,
        clutching the hot vein of your cell phone

as you drive your mother in her conical straw hat
        across the bumpy Vermont fields,

staring out from her yolky Alzheimer's haze
        as the car lurches over the mud and leaves.

No one wants to challenge your story,
        you who never should have left Burma,

your loneliness first swelling
        high above Atlantic City

where you built your makeshift apocalyptic nest
        pulling in the cheapest Gods that flew around,

storm after storm in that neon grim city.
        Now your fingers bruise your rosary with mad devotion.

No one can weave as fiercely as you
        in your tattered white bathrobe,

gray roots frosting your scalp,
        peering out from the curtains

like a spider sensing its web pricked,
        wrapping each social worker

in the pure white gauze of your stories
        as they look at you with the tenderness

reserved for an infant or a dog
        and speak to you of boundaries,

calling you back to the steamy jungles of your birth
        where you ran and ran through the night

and woke to a python wrapped around a tree
        your father hacking its head off, prying

its 17-foot long body off the trunk.
        It took so long for it to die,

uncoil enough so you could feast on the eggs
        lined up like potatoes in its womb.

Let go of the steering wheel, just a little.
        Who is to say what suffocates, what heals,

coaxing yourself home each night,
        as you're hurled through space

landing with a thump,
        into the great American refugee hive to begin

this frantic human work, perpetual manic revival,
        stretching your way through the half-light
                of this vast unraveling strangeness?

## Bus Station, Kampala, Uganda
For Will, age 3


We are lost.

Holding you tight,
    the drunks pawing me

as I weave through the stalls
    sticky with beer and urine

looking for a way to get us out.
    Gray buses wheeze over the colossal potholes,

barnacles of street kids
    clinging to their sides.

I don't know if you know it,
    but we are winding through alleys

where dogs bleed from their butts,
    a freshly pummeled woman

lies like pounded meat in the gutter,
    reeling from the punches for requesting a condom,

or if you hear the gurgle that is blood in her cheek
    as she slumps into a puddle

while the drunken crowd jeers.
    Meanwhile, back at the Lake Victoria hotel,

the hibiscus lashes its red
    tongue into the cool night,

wealthy *muzungus** spread their stiff white napkins
    starched and white as calla lilies.

Hush, sweet boy,
    swollen broken nests of these slums,

I can hardly breathe
    but for the rotting and the birthing.

For now, cooing, clueless, you can hardly see the difference
    between the squashed condom

the man threw at her in disgust and the crushed
    lily flattened by the *muzungu*'s high heel,

between the bleeding, the bleeding from everywhere there is an opening
    and the languid arch of the red hibiscus
        sprawled against the night.

**muzungu* means "white person" in East Africa.

## Lady's-slipper, Red Eft

As a child I awoke
to the furiousness of bees.

All morning my mother and I combed the woods
for red efts, trout lily, trillium.

I learned young
the smell of God and soil.

The first time I saw a lady's-slipper
I felt embarrassed, the pink-veined pouches,

simultaneously ephemeral and genital,
floating toad-balloons,

half scrotum, half fairy,
half birth, half death.

Without the formalities of church and school,
lust and spirit first came to me

as one
through the potent hips of spring.

But flowers, like fear, once inside me
never lay still

amidst my restless
stalking of the woods,

I wanted something bulky to thank,
to name, to explain all the impossible grace.

So I dragged my thirsty body
over the hills, into the trees.

I let the plump red efts, orange fingers tiny as rain,
crawl across my neck, onto my cheek,

half reptile, half elf,
half earth, half magic.

Years passed,
spring after spring cycled through me,

again and again I arrived in heaven
through touch,

lust, even, for the wrinkled pouches of lady's-slipper,
the soft lemon-bellied efts

that waddled pigeon-toed across my palm.
Now I walk my daughter through April's black mud.

It's been a long winter,
she hasn't quite unfurled.

Still, she sticks her ear into the cacophony of crows
above us, the way a dog sniffs

at a tight current of scent.
Across the meadow the peepers

gossip in their giant cities,
salamanders toddle

over the black soil,
back into the cold ponds they think of as mother.

*awake, awake*

*what if, what if*

What if God is walking through us,
picking seasons, histories, humans off himself

like milkweed from a sweater,
wading through us,

a slow giant through warm ponds,
feeling the odd tickle of religions

like tangled weeds at his feet?
I watch Ana now in full bloom,

despite the rain, running outside barefoot,
setting up dolls' nests in the fields,

collecting moles, covering them in leaves,
naming them even though they're dead.

She skitters across the garden, singing,
she too is learning young

the restlessness of rapture,
the way beauty is hard to sit with,
the way it bends the body into prayer,
the way ripeness must be touched.

Soft black earth of the garden,
she and her brother all fists and toes.

I watch her digging into heaven—
soil, toads, bulbs, buds,

the craning neck of spring—
and all summer

the sweet long green meadows.

# Mud

## *(Vermont/South Sudan)*

The pond black and bulging,
    twigs, branches poking from the water
like the stiff feet of, dare I say, fallen soldiers.

I drag whole limbs onto shore,
    globs of frog eggs surface like transparent brains,
Ana cupping the dimpled jelly,
    the dogs licking it like caviar.
Entranced, she squeezes it,
    while Will plunks his toes into a fleet of tadpoles,
cold mud sucking his foot into its mouth.

I tell myself it's not violence
    but overeager love,
this lust with which they squeeze the living.

Meanwhile, the rains just started in Juba, South Sudan,
    making travel near impossible.
Still my husband pushes a saggy jeep for eight hours
    through four feet of mud, a Sudanese boy
lying unconscious in the back seat.
    The jeep rocking and lurching
on the only road cleared of mines
    as my husband tries to inch it forward, this, his own labor of love,
like birth, like sex, something always tears,
    his foot jammed with a thorn as he heaves and sinks
his toenail tearing off, until even he gives up
    and forces them to turn back,
still 40 miles from Aliab, the whole village waiting,
    caught in an outbreak of cholera,
its one river littered with rusty ammunition,
    trucks large as elephants lying on their sides.

When Abraham, their Lost Boy, came home after 18 years
    the elders sacrificed a white cow.
Jump over it, into peace, they cried
    while the women tipped their thin necks back,
their whips of ululation uncoiling in the heat.

A day later, I find a frog shrunken in the corner of the bathroom
    but still breathing. I race it to the pond,
children running confused behind me,
    watch it sink, stunned, still dried and wrinkled,
like Abraham, now more American than Sudanese,
    sitting wide-eyed and stiff amidst the wailing and singing.

At dusk, the peepers scream themselves into existence,
    Ana and Will, draped in raincoats
run like drunken tents across the field.

When I catch up, Ana is horrified—
    two male frogs griplocked onto a female,
her flesh bulging between the swollen buds of their fingers.

And it occurs to me, how I came to be married to this man,
    I followed him from country to country,
gripped him hard as the frogs—
    Still he did not pry me off, as I have tried to do
with his overeager love, for this gangly country of South Sudan.
    Who knows what will be torn next,
    as he moves blindly, but well-intentioned,
        amidst the irresistible mud?

## The Crow

I saw a crow once,
pecking at the wild ferment of our compost,
a frenzy of black wing and beak, squawk and relish,
bouncing across the soggy geography.
It looked up, a little guilty,
as it gulped down something orange and nubile.
Nectar flecked across its throat,
it kept pumping its brittle wings, nervous but euphoric,
dancing almost, over the ripe warm pile,
digging its claws into the juicy terrain.
And suddenly I knew how war
must feel on the earth's beleaguered back,
the constant pecking,
the restless itching armies,
the wince and smart, gush and heave of old arguments dug up
as the earth lunges through blue space,
overripe tomatoes seeping down its back
as it holds its place in the orbit,
hoping someday to shake it all off, like a dog after a swim,
the humans smattering like droplets into the galaxy,
evolution a bit surprised,
but adjusting itself politely
and beginning the long haul once more.

## Indra's Net

*Suspended above the palace of Indra is an enormous net that extends infinitely in all directions. A brilliant jewel is attached to each of the knots of the net. Each jewel contains and reflects the image of all the other jewels in the net, which sparkles in the magnificence of its totality. (The Avatamsaka Sutra)*


We mothers meet on the playground, sun-hungry,
       kicking at scabs of ice,
shuffling and bumping tired phrases against each other,
       all too broken by winter
              to say how things really are.

The bell rings,
    I wave to my daughter, small magician,
all enigma, moon and mercury,
    shifting alchemy of low blood sugar,
Harry Potter, and Dutch DNA,
all day her mood refracting and reflecting
    the whims of the queen bees
in her first-grade hive.

She labors into the car,
    hauling her Sisyphean pink knapsack
    stuffed with assessments and assignments,
        endless trelliswork of No Child Left Behind
    around which the billion strands of her imagination
        are trained to weave.

Sometimes we don't have time to do better
    I say to myself in the car,
wincing at my generic query about her day,
    she faithfully delivering her monosyllabic answer
        as we drive home through the whirling snowflakes,
our stale comments lacing and braiding together
    as we reach from front seat to back,

between the jewels of mouths and eyes,
    tired word stitched to tired word,

this ritual of rough encapsulations
    of infinite reflections upon infinite reactions,
our mouths the blinking cheap motels of the stars and heavens
    still, a noble kind of reaching,
a dogged kind of loving,
    weaving its own coarse net
through the gleaming fields of winter.

## Borders

The phone rings,
you're there, all sun, war and heat.
You've decided to drive
over the Ugandan border,
the jeep all rigged—
it's a done deal,
but I beg anyway.
Nairobi's slums burned,
ports closed, no gasoline,
so you fill up with what you can get,
strap the jeep with tools and jerrycans.

In the morning
our daughter hovers at my bedroom door
lunar and rumpled,
she must have overheard me on the phone
pleading.

Silently she assumes her throne
over the heater,
plots her revolution,
the warm air puffing her white nightgown
like a Queen Toad.

She reading me, reading her.

When her brother Will
tries to share her space
she jabs him hard in the ribs,
anger spilling red down her face and chest.

And it happens again,
whereby war, however diluted, however transformed,
however many times removed, has spread,

whereby the suffering of Kenya begets Uganda,
begets my husband,
begets me, begets Ana, begets her brother...

Later in the mudroom, getting ready for school
I see Will kick our tiny old mutt.

Perhaps it will end here, with this dog
who pees all over the house,
sleeping on the couch all day long,
cataracts like clouded moons,
for now, noble keeper of the passing flame.

The school bus arrives,
my children chatter,
emptied of their small wars
they skip lightly toward its open door,
the dog limping eagerly behind.

# Beneath the Sky, the Longing
*(Thimphu, Bhutan)*

At the top of the Thimphu hills, sun leaves its afterbirth everywhere,
    prayer flags drench the pines,
        a monk scampers away like a red fox,

couples park their cars,
    condom wrappers lodged doggedly in the mud,
        asserting their rightful place in the path to enlightenment,

dingy Indian buses, painted gaudy as prostitutes
    careen around the battered road to the capital,
        taking villagers to Thimphu, where lust for the West huddles like fog,

packs of roaming boys dressed in black jeans and t-shirts
    scour the streets for drugs, the ones who eye the Westerners hungrily,
        black eyes nibbling feverishly at the manic commercials

flashing from the storefront TVs,
    the ones who failed their exams, left their farms,
        sitting hungover at the dingy youth center, unemployed,

confessing their uselessness to the Welsh monk
    who has made it his life to work with these boys, gutted and global now,
        to bring them back into the fold.

Meanwhile, tucked above the cobbled streets
    in the smoky Thimphu disco,
        CNN shouts its noble manifesto from its perch above the bar,
schools of ghostly expats sway,
    waving their drunken limbs,
        lightheaded, wan from this geography of bliss,

still, they lay their drunken bodies down on the stiff hotel beds,
    all night they try and let it go and let it go,
        and still they come back to this density of longing,

hard kernel of desire where the bulky psyche chips its tooth,
      and winces again,
            stumbling back to the breath.

Outside their window barking dogs mince the night till it bleeds,
      the Bhutanese boy, high on meth,
            wailing a kind of love song for the West
                  deep in the alley below.

## Opening Day, Mukaya
### (New Sudan Secondary School for Girls)


All day we wait
        for the moist gills of night to open,
                croak and squawk of frogs, lizards,
bats soaring over the tent
        land with a splash in the mango tree,
                clutching and sucking the glorious fruit.

We have arrived again
        through the screeching heat of day,
                sun stripping the fields violently like a bed.

Planet of Mars, planet of fire and war.

Even grief, escaping the sun's manic inquisition,
        waits to swell.
                For three nights the eerie death drumming for a toddler
                    pummels our tent like rain.

Like missionaries staring from the toy plane
        swallowing the vast expanse of Sudan
                we are dropped onto the earth,

and begin the drive, whole jaws of road gaping open,
        van rebirthing through mud hole after hole.

Chiefs arrive for the ceremony in their Salvation Army clothes,
        battered cowboy hats. Not the tall stalks of fierce Dinka,
                but old men tamed by war, rising up on their wobbly canes
                    in this nursing home post-war Sudan has become.

For six hours we sit through their sedating oration,
  wives lassoing us back from sleep
    with their fierce whips of ululation.

Dingy shantytown of tents where the hired help lives,
  a deer strains its tether, two mangy puppies wrestle,
    goat limbs hang from a branch.

Women squat, poke at the coals,
  feathers stuck to their hands, hair,
    white chickens thrown like pom-poms in the dirt.

And we don't know how they take it, the stirring and tending
  of their daily cauldrons of meat and blood,
    the war still raw inside them.

We say our goodbyes to the new school girls lying
  under their mosquito nets like captive brides,
    rows of bunkbeds, this their new life,

of education, three meals a day, the word has spread,
  as far as Wau and Aweil, girls from around the county
    on the backs of motorcycles

skirts tucked up, tin luggage on their heads,
  military convoys winding their way
    around the gutted mines,

filled with female cargo bumping, jostling, giggling,
  this their opening day, fierce reckoning,
    spilling their futures across the pockmarked soil

        like milk, fire, rain.

# From Heaven, Mother Theresa Looks Down on Daya Dan
### (Daya Dan Orphanage, Missionaries of Charity, Calcutta)

> "(For Westerners), Calcutta becomes the Disneyland of suffering."
> —McKenzie Wark

Without her glasses, they were just a stream from West to East,
    each day the waves, lapping over and over
        onto the shores of Daya Dan.

Focused, she could see them, ponytailed, sandaled,
    all patchouli and caged nerves,
        toting their ratty green knapsacks, grungy journals,

emerging from the taxis, bone-tired
    hauling their boulders of guilt up the crumbling stairs.
        And though they say they are not Catholic

over and over they baptize themselves,
    bending into the bodies that litter the cribs,
        wincing at the small, clingy deaths in midstream,

rising up with another twisting, sticky child,
    then laying them down, kneading the gnarled bodies
        that refuse to flatten, muscles stiff as pipe.

Even after the monsoon takes its heavy skirts elsewhere,
    still they come, dogged through the swollen heat,
        tall hungry ghosts, paddling after the nuns, sheepish and sweaty.

Go home, she'd sometimes tell them,
    but still they'd dunk themselves in India's dying,
        coming up for air, dunking themselves again,

the toddlers turning toward them,
    whole fields restless and rebellious for touch.
        Mary, the oldest orphan, still there after all these years,

sitting like a queen, perusing her kingdom of cribs,
        holding court with her sweat-drenched devotees
                who found her at Howra train station

dragging her legless torso on the Calcutta Times,
        limping monkey trailing behind her.
                On hot days, gently hosing her down, avoiding

the leaking plum where pigeons made a meal of her eye.
        This is how it goes at Daya Dan,
                the nuns starched stiff with Christ,

tying a defiant toddler to a crib,
        barking their orders to the Westerners,
                wet-eyed and overwhelmed, dripping with Christ,

winding their capes of doubt through the muggy faiths of others,
        covered with the lint of Asian Gods
                stumbling up the steps,

toward the crippling call of the Adoration
        pulling them from afar, like a lost love,
                like a former aching life perhaps sloughed off too soon,

and they, awkwardly joining in,
        their voices rising to the ceiling,
                gently weaving the infinite, the way birds weave sky

not knowing until now, amidst their long march,
        their righteous, lonely theologies,
                the ecstasy of being humble, of being no one, of bowing their heads.

Mother Theresa knew they had been pierced with God's love, not any other God
        but God the Father, whether or not they approved,
                whether or not they wanted to let Him in.

Then back to their chores,
the scrubbing of floors, laundry, plates.
Just as it should be, just as it must be.

## Milk
*(Sudanese Refugee Camp, Northwest Uganda)*


I.
Our drivers gun insanely over the dusty, red roads,
    lurching from pothole to pothole.
        Caravan of slick, adrenalized vans,

tattooed with symbols of western aid,
    Will on my lap, trying to nurse between bumps,
        my hands a helmet to his bobbing skull.

A three-legged goat hobbles to the side,
    and though we imagine we are a huge interruption,
        women balancing jerrycans on their heads
        face our wake of dust and rage

as they would any other gust of wind—

*Water, sun, NGO.*

We arrive covered in orange dust, coughing,
    fleet of SUVs parked under the trees,
        engines cooling, Star Trekian cockpits flashing,

alarms beeping and squawking as we zip-lock them up
    and leave them black-windowed, self-contained as UFOs.

Behind the gate, we stumble through the boiling, shoulder-deep sun,
    Will and I trying to play soccer
        as a trickle of Sudanese kids crosses the road

hanging against the fence, watching the chubby *muzungu* boy
    I've toted around Africa like a pot of gold.
        Three years old, he knows they're watching, so he does a little dance,
            his Spider Man shoes lighting up as they hit the dust.

II.
Part African bush, part Wild West,
    we're based in Arua, grungy, dusty frontier town,
        giant dieseled trucks barrel through, spreading their wake of adrenalin,
           obese sacks of grain lying like walruses
           inside.

    I chase Will from malarial puddle to puddle,
        white blouse frilled like a gaudy gladiolus,
          lavish concern for my chubby son
           suddenly rococo, absurd.


III.
7-foot giants of the SPLA, huddle together, drinking,
    talking Dinka politics, repatriation, the New Sudan,
        wives lanky as giraffes set food on the table
          and move slowly away.

In candlelight the men's forehead scars gleam,
    I flutter, acting more deferential than I'm used to,
        slowly I'm learning Sudanese grammar:

men are the verbs; women, the conjunctions that link them together.

In the thick of rain we walk home,
    Ugandans huddled under their makeshift bird cages,
        Will now pointing to the basic vocabulary of this road:

dead snake, prickly bush, squealing pig, peeing child.
    Three drunk men sit under a shack,
        scrape the whiteness off us as we walk by.

Though I don't want to hear it,
    though I love Africa,
it starts up anyway, the milky mother cells of my body high-fiving,
my mind quietly repeating the story of my son's lucky birth,
    his rich American inheritance.

IV.
My husband drops into bed, dragging a thick cloak of requests.
      All day, I've labored behind him, toting our clueless *muzungu,*
            watching him, dogged Dutchman in his rubber clogs

climbing the soggy hills of Kampala, despite the noonday heat,
      a posse of hopeful Lost Boys following him,
          he, afraid of nothing, really, not even death,
             me afraid of everything really, most of all his death.

In the distance, trucks rev up to cross the bush
      where Sudanese families perched like kites caught in trees,
         wait for the next shipment.

But it's night now,
      the three of us inside the cloud chamber of our mosquito net,
         the two of them breathing, safe.

Will's nursing again, though he doesn't need to,
      swelling like a tick
         and though I don't want to love
   the sweet mists of our tiny tent home,
   the lush wetlands of our lives,
         its thick rope bridges and gentle Ugandan hills,

the fat claw of my heart rises up,
      fertile, lucky, random
         pulsing and hissing its victory song.

## Lost Boy
For Gabriel Panther Ayuen


Panther sits inside his apartment,
heat cranked up to 80, curtains closed,
a pile of chicken boiling on the stove,
slides another Kung Fu movie into the VCR,
settles back into the smelly,
swaybacked couch, a Budweiser between his legs.
He giggles.
In half an hour he'll ride his bike
to Walmart, round stray shopping carts
from the cracked gray lot,
crashing them back into their steel corrals.

At first they dropped by all the time,
the church ladies, the anthropologists,
the students, the local reporter.
They all left elated, having found something real,
like yoga and organic food.

The first Thanksgiving, three families booked him.
Leaning hungrily across
the long white table,
they nibbled at his stories,
his lean noble life.
Over and over he told them about lions,
crocodiles, eating mud and urine.

He remembers joining
a black river of boys,
their edges swelling and thinning
as they wound their way
over the tight-lipped soil, sun stuck to their backs.
He remembers dust mushrooming up
around a sack of cornmeal as it thudded
and slumped over, like a fat woman crying in the sand.

And the Americans came alive, with a sad,
compassionate glow, a kind of sunset inside them.

When he got off the plane
the church ladies took him to a store,
bought him fresh sneakers
soft and white as wedding cake.
The next day he walked through whole aisles of dog food.
Two years later, November again,
he's dropped out of high school—
he can't take
the kids staring, the tiny numbers and letters
he can't keep straight,
the basketball team he didn't make
despite his famous height.

Now he looks like a too-tall gangster,
all gold-chained and baggy-trousered.
The church ladies give him hushed looks:
*we regret to inform you, the path you've taken is not what we had hoped for.*

He's channel-surfing,
listening to Bob Marley on his Walkman,
his long legs awkwardly pushed out
to each side, the way giraffes
split their stilts
to drink water.
Africa's moved inside him now,
all cramped and bored, sleeping a lot.

He cracks another beer
starts to float,
the reggae flooding the vast blue-black continent
of his body draped like a panther
over the sides of the sofa.

His cousin calls, she needs more money,
her son has malaria. She can't afford school fees anymore.
His uncle gets on the phone to remind him to study hard,
come back and build a new Sudan.

Later he stumbles into the bathroom
to brush his teeth, inside him
groggy Africa flinches at the neon light,
paces, then settles in the corner
of its den, paws pushing into the walls
of his ribs with a dull pain.

The next morning he wakes,
stubborn Africa still shoved up against his ribs,
refusing to roll over, into the middle
of himself where he can't feel it anymore,
into some open place
where he ends
and America finally begins.

# Young West Meets My East
*(India)*

## I. Dharamsala

Eight hours we drive north—
heat, dust, corrugated tin shacks,
pot-holed manic streets.
Schizzed-out dogs weave the alleys.
In the garbage heaps, dung-crusted cows
sway like blimps over a litter of puppies.

We hit the quarries,
whole families squatting, smashing rocks,
men in white diapers, shoulder blades stuck out like wings.
Five-year-old Ana, wilted, presses her face into my thigh.

Daybreak and we're still winding up the foothills,
our sleepy driver finally stops for chai.
Across the street a group of lepers wave their heads about like seals,
shifting back and forth on their stunted limbs,
and I'm off again, launching into another sermon on injustice.

Deep in the slums, I study her eyes, what they're drawn to,
the Pepsi ads, the one dusty Barbie doll
straddling Ganesh like a freak.

We arrive in Dalai Lama-land,
the crush of crowds freak her out.
From the balcony, she sits with her white rice and boiled egg
watching the red capillaries of monks
scurrying toward His Holiness' teachings—

it's true,
everything has a beauty, if watched from afar.

But I want her to get closer.

## II. Jammu

Avalanches in Srinegar, highways closed,
at the airport a near riot starts over who will board.
I push her forward, like an offering,
blond hair, planetary eyes,
and we're shuffled by the stewardess
to the head of the crowd
while the lines of weary men look on
and accept their fate.


## III. Goa

I slink around the fancy hotel ashamed,
while Ana springs to life,
moving from wellspring to wellspring,
swimming pool, cornflakes, cable TV.

But the way she dims her delight when I'm looking,
as if she mustn't relish this
too much in front of me.

In fresh white dresses
we step barefoot down the marble staircase,
into the catacombs of spa rooms,
New Age music hovers like a ghost in the halls,
scented candles spread the hotel's version of The Orient.

Finally some Westernized-India she'll try,
we're all over the Henna.
She sticks out her chubby hand, ready to be painted.
For now I vow I'll be more patient with this child.

## IV. Vermont

It's spring again,
mud rising, caked and grubby.
I whistle for our overfed dogs;
two small hippos bounce cluelessly across the snow-spotted fields,
tags jingling against the tin bowls as they devour their daily ration.
I can't resist—
*Remember the slaves, Ana? They get less food than this.*
She looks at me irritably, my East and her West grating.
So I sit with her, and chatter,
luring her back in with an offer
of mac and cheese.

I think of Nepalese selling their daughters for new tin roofs,
the fetid cages of the brothels where they are penned.
Ulan Bator, the camel peeing on the family's prize satellite dish,
it's bleak, sober spring, the smell of beer and MTV,
Bhutan with its 40 new glossy TV channels.

So many Easts leaning so eagerly West.

The sun sets, fog lifts humbly off the mountain's back,
she tinkers with her American Girl doll.
The maples tapped, soon it will be boiling time,
the shacks fired up, glowing and gushing like dragons,
the cloud chambers of sweet steam settling deep in her veins.

Sweet child,
her whole young life
I have pushed her past this mountain, past these clouds,
into foreign lands,
and though she does not wish to hear the brutal sounds
of their groping and clashing,
hungry cultures spread across each other,
mixing and merging in unequal combinations, as they always have,
and she does not yet know
        what to make of them.

## Before His Execution, God Looks Down on a Yoga Class

They told Him
He could have
one last look
before the long walk down the hall
into the viewing chamber, to be strapped
with fifty straps, the injection starting at exactly
10:15.

In solitary for 300 years,
when He asked the guard
what to expect, she laughed, only saying
the New Age has arrived, the Old Testament stamped out.

So he shuffled His feet along,
feeling effeminate in His light blue prison slippers,
hands chained behind His back,
the fluorescent lights barking in His face.

In the chamber, He took a breath,
stepped forward
and peered out onto the great vast space,
the cosmos with its sullen orange and pink mists, the planets
hanging quietly as spiders.  And there it was,
Earth,
its bald swirled head
its whirling cacophony,

the guard nudged Him,
giving Him the prison binoculars.

The yoga class:
That they were all women was no surprise,
they had always given Him the most grief,
all they did was bitch bitch bitch
toward the end of His rule.

Many times He had tried to touch them,
but they'd always squat in fear, looking dumb, leaking like toads.
    But then He could never help Himself,
and it had come to this, they had moved on
to the New Age, and he could not help
but see their beauty, these masses of hope,
these sea plants, sacro-tropic.
No one told Him they would look so graceful,
that His mouth would sag when they began to pray,
slow and fluid as underwater ballet,
their bodies like tendrils curling up and out,
deep sea vines reaching, uncurling like fiddleheads in unison.

No one had prepared him

for the sea of white bodies below
shifting from asana to asana, a flight of birds, a school of fish,

pushing up toward some other God,

that they might flourish best here, in this liminal,
moist place between dogma and creed, that unlike vines,
they did not need a stake
in order to grow.

Taking a step back, He tried to gather himself, but
could not help
but look again at the field of bodies
below, lying now in corpse pose, *savasana*,
bellies rising and falling,
incense thick as fog,
thoughts floating off like milkweed.

As they strapped Him down
He licked the spittle from His lower lip,
His own death now an empty pasture no
one would visit.

He only wanted the white bodies swaying
like a field of flowers beneath Him to touch His
clenched jaw, to soften it just this once

and for the first time in His whole long life
He knew what shame was, he ached and ached,
He knew what it felt like
to be human.

He began to unfurl.

*The Hunger Sutras: From Above, God and Buddha Look Down on the Earth from the Hospital for Sick, Endangered and Arrested Gods*

### I. What God Saw

In the hospital La-Z-Boy
    sucking on the mints that calmed him down
God sat for a while
    rubbing his thumb
over the soft padded soles
    of the remote.
Hovering over the highways and church supermarkets
    of the late 20th century,
there was not much that interested Him now,
    this postmodern era with its
nervous cultures that
    shifted directions suddenly,
trying to fool their prey.
    Cocky humans, junked-up on speed,
all night revving their engines,
    skidding away from Truth.

The earth's been had, he told the Buddha,
filled with freaks and atheists.

Scanning the earth, he found Lily,
    tucked into the Lower East Side,
rubbing her rosary raw.

Lately, she confessed,
    when her baby suckled,
his plump hand fluttering over the hills
    of her open breasts,
landing and relanding delicate
    and yet clumsy as a toy airplane,

she felt her spine tingle,
    as if it were carbonated. And when his slack mouth slid off her nipple,
his head hanging heavy as a planet,
    the drops of milk inching down her ribs
like small spiders, she felt her skin's surface
    pucker with goosebumps, freezing and melting.

Once already she had turned herself in to the police
    for licking the white tulips
in front of the Korean groceries,
    the buds heavy as cold eggs in her hand.
She could not resist them. So she buried them like canaries
    in shoeboxes from Sears.

After her confession they let her stay for the night,
    not knowing where else to put her.

The next morning God awoke, early,
    nudged the guard
and paid him for the binoculars.

In a cold cell, He found Lily,
    tense with disinfectant, her body
white and stiff as old bread,
    rigged so tight she couldn't move,
the blood of Christ swelling from her,
    earnest as red geraniums.


## II. What the Buddha Saw

With its bulging ring he almost mistakes it for Saturn.
      Billions of egos, clumped like caviar
around the midsection of the earth.
      In Thailand, a throng of saffron-robed monks
      looks like a smear of mustard
caught on the sleeve of the earth.

In New York, a pale, thin girl meditates fiercely,
        her spine stiff as a skyscraper,
her aim impeccable, her thoughts shot immediately
        upon release. The more she kills
the more the thoughts come,
        until finally she rises from her cushion in disgust.

A Zen monk sits in a high security prison
        teaching inmates to meditate.
Flocks of pigeons peck at the same old ground of thought,
        guilt, redemption, redemption, guilt,
until a bell rings, and they disperse,
        only to resettle, and peck again,
the mind's floor bleeding from their beaks.

A woman paces her deck at sunset,
        her thoughts pawing the horizon like a cat toying
with a dying bird, loneliness stretched inside her body
        pink and raw as tuna.
Each night she swallows another sunset with her vodka,
        a thick slab of sadness lodged
like a beached whale in her mind,
        waves of reassurance
unable to pull its bloated body from the sand.

So much suffering.

Still, how beautiful they are
        even when they fret and curse,
and in between the thoughts, like small birds,
        instinctively opening their mouths
            toward sky.

# Dinka Bible

*One morning after the crucifixion, a Sudanese boy came to see his mother and father. He found his hut burnt to the ground. Two figures dressed in white asked him, "Boy, why are you weeping?" "Because," he replied, "they have taken away my family, and I do not know where they have laid them."*


The first Sunday
his host mother took him to church
in the town where Snowflake Bentley discovered
that each snowflake has a unique design.
Black leather boots crusted with salt,
she gunned up the frozen hill,
truck wheezing like a stuck pig,
Achak clinging, afraid he'd fly out,
into the mute, white fields.

She figured he might as well get used to it,
the snow, the cold,
so she pulled over, next to some steaming cows,
*Scoop it up*, she said, grinning,
his skinny fingers springing back in horror.

She told him the Bible
would heal him from his trauma,
he would make God's word his own, in this new land,
as humans had done for centuries.
He pictured spreading its noble words,
back in Sudan, in a new suit and tie,

until then, the loneliness must lay quiet,
lining his heart like lichen, like frost,
as he stocked the shelves with dog food.

Arriving late,
pale eyes staring,

thick pink hands working the hymnal,
perfume stinging the walls of his nose,
the words of the Bible sliding over his brain
fast, too fast, just as he caught one,
others fell on top
in a heap he could not unscramble.

After the service, powdered doughnuts crouch
like small rabbits in their boxes,
his host mother wipes the sugar off his mouth,
marking him as her own.

He sits on the couch,
and breaks into a sweat.
Fat ladies smelling like diapers, notice,
and pat his damp skull,
until he catapults out of the land of good intentions
and throws up outside.

In the black of night,
he hears nothing
except for the crunch, crunch
of his host mother's boots,
coming to raise him up
*coming for to carry him home.*

And he knew how lonely Mary must have felt
when she came upon Jesus' empty tomb,
this pockmarked country, cold as moon,
the stones rolled back from the *muzungu's* eyes,
the black holes everywhere.

# War Metaphysics for a Sudanese Girl

For Aciek Arok Deng

I leave the camp, unable to breathe,

me Freud girl, after her interior,
she "Lost Girl," after my purse,

her face:
dark as eggplant,
her gaze:
unpinnable, untraceable,
floating, open, defying the gravity
I was told keeps pain in place.

Maybe trauma doesn't harden,
packed tight as sediment at the bottom of her psyche,
dry and cracked as the desert she crossed,
maybe memory doesn't stalk her
with its bulging eyes.

Once inside the body, does war move up or down?
Maybe the body pisses it out,
maybe it dissipates, like sweat and fog
under the heat of yet another colonial God?

In America, we say, "Tell us your story, Lost Girl
you'll feel lighter,
it's the memories you must expel,
the bumpy ones, the tortures, the rapes, the burnt huts."

So Aciek brings forth all the war she can muster,
and the doctors lay it on a table, like a stillbirth,
and pick through the sharpest details
bombs, glass, machetes
and because she wants to please them

she coughs up more and more,
dutifully emptying the sticky war
like any grateful Lost Girl in America should
when faced with a flock of white coats.

This is how it goes at the Trauma Center:
all day the hot poultice of talk therapy,
coaxing out the infection,
at night, her host family trying not to gawk,
their veins pumping neon fascination,
deep in the suburbs, her life flavoring dull *muzungu* lives,
spicing up supper, really,
each Lost Girl a bouillon cube of horror.

## Attiak Refugee Camp, Northern Uganda

Thatched huts ferment,
men slump, drinking *kongo* till they float,
sleeping through boredom,
peeing out wasted time,
lisping and burping through stories
about when they were in control.

Meanwhile the women,
sensing a lull in the status quo,
push to the surface as the Masters fall—
carrying water, firewood, thatching grass
queen bees in this malarial hive,
relieving each other as they wait in thick, twisting lines
for rations the men will sell for beer.

For the first time in years, the UNHCR reports,
women in the camp report wife beating has declined.

# Lord's Resistance Army
*(Northern Uganda)*


## I.  Capture

First the shea nut oil,
        on the forehead, chest, back, hands and feet,
sign of the cross,
        separating them from mother and father.

In the lineup, girls choose a husband by picking a shirt
        from a pile on the ground.
In the bush, they fetch water, assemble the guns,
        carry the commander's chairs, soda, cassava.

Under a tree they sleep, tending the fires,
        drinking weeds and boiled sorghum.
Some nights Kony wakes them to pray, bare-chested in the rain,
        the next day they do not have sex
or cook with oil from the *yao* tree.

At night, they raid a village in Lira,
        sign of the cross on their chest, forehead and guns,
looking for children
        big enough to hold a machete,
small enough to creep through windows.

They try not to take two children from one hut.


## II.  Rehab

A blond-haired man in a robe reads the gospel,
        sewing up their botched pasts parable by parable,
wincing as the thread of Christ
        slides through a swollen memory

and a crisscross of stitches from another God's land
        patchworks their psyches back together again.

All night bad things dart in and out of their minds
        like fish.


### III.  Mato Oput

*The Oput tree produces a highly bitter herb, which, in drinking, symbolizes the swallowing of the horror of war.*

Sound of the cicada, grating teeth.
The commander drinks the bitter herb,
admits his guilt, pushes forth a sickly goat in return,
his daughter scuffling forward,
both of them now sipping from a calabash.

The chiefs smash the egg, throw down the *opobo*,
yell hard, *step over it, into peace.*

All day the women and their rebel babies
stand in a line of 400
smushing their infant's right foot into the raw egg,
this their child's first baptism into the tail end of war.
Goats trailing gingerly behind them
licking the sticky yolk from their heels,
the *muzungu* with his monkey camera
dodging in and out of the crowd.

Deep in the bush, their sisters still get distributed like shoes,
cycles charted for maximum fertility,
and when they limp home, womb full of Kony's progeny,
villagers once jealous of their innocence,
hiss    *r e b e l s*    as they pass.

## The Sweet Hereafter

It seems I am no monk.
It turns out, I cannot sit with suffering
without saddling it with an ill-fitting God.

Who knows what tipped me over,
another Christmas and its neon grin,
the living dead at Walmart
pushing their loaded carts through the aisles,
the class I taught on child soldiers in Uganda,
the way the Lord's Resistance Army kidnaps boys
forcing them to beat another child to death; each day
a new boy in the camp chosen. I sat there, after the lecture,
wondering what happens to the body:
is it pounded like steak until it is limp and soft,
and how do they kill a child with such small fists and feet?
As the boy looks up through the pummeling, does he
see a kind of God waiting for him, smiling?
Does he know instinctively, like the bee
and the hummingbird, how to find nectar?

I need to know—
one day, will it happen, will I swallow a God who can handle all of this,
my eyes watering as I hold Him down?
Will the gasoline in my throat
turn to wine
and I feel warm and giddy,
sitting in the front pew of the Church of the Holy Light,
the sun's giant paw resting on my back?

In spring,
my mother will die,
I will smell another impossibly thick
fist of cherry blossom.
When I take her body into the woods,

when I think I can't take the loss, the light fading,
and I sink to my knees, will there be a God
hovering, or will a God surface from within?

What I want is this:
after they lower her body into the earth
and I hear fear
whimpering in its crib,
I won't believe my good fortune
when a God kicks in
and lets down His rain of reassurance,
and I sit in awe,
like the first time my milk came in,
and I lay there
in the moss,
        my whole blouse sopping.

## Christmas Eve, Kampala, Uganda

Compost city, neon slumyard, Britney Spears
rising above the sticky bar,
buses from Juba coughing and belching,
inching slow as whales in the darkness
while the red-butted monkeys in the bush
leap from branch to branch.
Here, under fluorescent lights,
rat-dogs sniff the streets like addicts,
Dinka soldiers mumble,
drag their HIV around in a haze,
while skimpy girls gawk at televisions
till the manager waves them away like flies.
Still the moon, creamy and subdued,
spreads its patient lunar gauze over all of them,
not just the *muzungus* working off their Western guilt,
the noble golden cheetahs,
or the Doctors Without Borders,
but the limp jaw of the glue sniffer too,
the sprawled belly of the wife beater,
and the drunken man
sitting in a corner
working his cock into a frenzy
as his groans stretch wide with defeat
into some warm swatch
of the moon's sweet milk.

Oh holy tenderness of this mute misty planet,
bless these fragile, harried nests
the tired and hungry build.

## Email Elegy

*Dedicated to emails from Save Darfur, War Child, Africa Action, Amnesty International, Human Rights Watch, Free the Slaves, AIDS Action, Doctors Without Borders, Africa ELI*


How quietly they land,
      bits of global sorrow accumulating like snowfall
          as I teach a class, attend a meeting,
             make a cup of tea.

What if early man wasn't designed
      for this downpour of international horrors?

Or maybe human evolution slogs through any weather,
      the nimble human psyche adapting,
          the violence at first like lightning to the brain,

then a stinging blizzard, and now a light rain,
      the damp, guilty silence left behind as we move almost nimbly
          from Haiti to Google, Facebook to Sudan.

The brain's cramped bardo
      stuffed with the strays of CNN,
          lining our million neural pathways, begging.

Shouldn't we bless them,
      the messages that flash into the Times Square of our brains
          amid the rapid multitasking?

Perhaps later they call to us,
      rising up like loons on the back pools of the mind,
          hinting at some remote part of us, raw and ragged,

when horror still stuck
      fresh as weeds to the skin.

## Moths

What to do with the giant moth
      caught in our tent on the last night, dive-bombing our headlamps?
I tell my daughter not to touch it,
      why, she says, you'll change them, I say,
trying to explain how our fingers are sponges
      for their blue and gold powders,
but we have no choice, she says
      as we pull down the tent and begin our journey home
watching them fly into the night
      only to flock to the bright light of the generator
whose haggard lungs we pump each night,
      a throng of cell phones and computers
plugged into its one beleaguered but outstretched vein,
      this global vein, neon river, with its flock of converts,
baptized in its current, this body electric
      just beginning to twist like the Nile
through the sweet green fields
      of the post-war south.

## To Market, to Market
*(Dharamsala, India, Tibetan Government in Exile)*


Tibetan boys cruise down to the square,
    scoping for Western girls studying Buddhism so earnestly
their hearts almost tear
    in the cool Himalayan air of this hill station

where boys flaunt their Orientalism when they need it most,
    tossing their glistening ponytails
like black rivers down their backs,

turning the switch of authenticity "on"
    like a neon sign that says OPEN for business,
black eyes hinting at the story
    of the frost-bitten trek through the mountains,

the ones the girls are dying to hear,
    girls in heat, pink and warm with the West,
moving in pockets of foreign chatter
    toward the nearest wifi café
where they'll split the beaks of their sleek laptops open
    succumb to the neon blue glow,
their eyes swimming as if underwater,
    in this glossy CNN planet.

For hours the boys stand outside,
    peering through the window, technotropic,
inching toward the shifting lights of the Wild West
    caught inside the screens

until finally the girls emerge,
    in the cold night, East and West circling each other,
the girls giggling,
    ready to fling the cramped purse of "the self"
onto the street and give themselves to everything.

Back in America, they feel empty in the numbed-out suburbs
    as they open their suitcases stuffed with prayer flags, beads,
buddhas, yak wool, other exotics from the Pureland
    they'll flaunt in the antsy college dorms,
the smell of incense and dirt releasing from them
    like an opiate their cells crave,
while across the globe, the Dalai Lama rises to meditate at 3 AM
    as the boys in Dharamsala dream their own thick myths,
clutching the girls emails white-knuckle tight
    long after they've fallen asleep.

## What to Give Her—A Confession

I.
Winter mornings,
you fumble down the stairs,
sink into my lap, groaning as you stretch
across my belly, draping yourself
over the sides of the chair.
I scan your face for the local weather
which will fill our house today,
bracing myself.
Still, I love your grumpiness
like I love the first grubby fists of spring.
Both have a right to be here.

Your green eyes won't hint at anything today,
glassy and self-contained, the way the planet Earth,
from a distance, has no mood.


II.
I confess
I have no religious home.
I've never had the luxury
of plunking you down into the velvet pews
of the blood-soaked Catholic church.
I confess
I have no Bible fat and smug as a toad
on my bedside table.

Days pass,
a little bit of Tibetan incense, a lot of winter solstice,
The Grinch Who Stole Christmas,
another time out,
another Jivamukti chant,
your brother bulldozing

down the buddhas you've lined
up at your shrine.

In our clumsy home of incense and dog hair,
I crave the weight of old cultures,
cranky and outdated as they can be.
I crave sediment,
whole layers of history upon us
like a wet blanket, but without the stink,
the itchy suffocation.

I confess
when you're hurting
I want you padded like a hockey player with gods
even death and doubt can't gnaw through.


III.
So tell me, little blonde one, this menagerie I've given you,
how do I know it's sticking—
are you getting enough red meat?

I am no pioneer,
tucked inside our house in rural Vermont
I don't want a patchwork quilt
I have to stitch alone at night
in the sometimes grace
sometimes loneliness
of the northeast kingdom.
And who knows if one gaping, stern God,
perched like a gargoyle above your bed,
wouldn't better weather the suffering
you know.

I confess at times I want to send you
into the bumpy flow of some massive pilgrimage,
while I rest, I promise, just for a little,

while the grandmothers, bread and stone soup
priestesses, crinkled hands dirty
from digging potatoes
hoist you up and dust you off.


IV.
Don't lose hope. We're not the only ones.
It's spring, I'm starting to spot them,
the other mothers staying up late at night,
isolated alchemists, tinkering, tinkering,
molding the clay of strange symbols,
spinning their own shaky looms of meaning
and the next day, offering them to their children
in the local churches we now call home.

## Yolk

Willy is determined
to make the wood duck eggs
hatch. I find them nestled
in the warm slack
of our sleeping dog's neck,
or inside a cardboard box next to his bed
in a nest of dish rags, light bulb
looming above like a screaming planet,
a sign etched in kindergarten scrawl
reminding us to be quiet.

They go where he does,
shuffling from room to room in his Batman slippers,
silent cold white globes
warmed by his grubby hands,
smuggled into school,
hidden in his fleece coat at the back
of his cubby.

We tell him the mother has left the nest for good,
who knows why,
perhaps we've scared her away?
Still, he loves the solemnity of the ritual,
the dire import of keeping them warm,
and we follow along
broken by his tenderness,
our own habitual tightness
starting to soften into the yolk
that the Buddhists say
is the ultimate nature of the heart.

When we found the eggs
at the side of the pond,
we broke one open,

wood duck fetus in its viscous coat,
already the noble dark fur, half solid, half vein
still feeding on the yolk.
And Willy staring right into it,
the way he always does with death,
never wincing at the clot of life
we place on the grass for the fox to gobble up.

# The Adoration

It's morning,
I pull you from the crib
all warm and yeasty,
your hair stuck up like two soft horns,
you beaming brighter than a headlight
in anticipation of the nip.

Silly boy,
tender pink niblet
succulent little beast,
waternut, love blossom,
*Panis bulbosa, lactata nippiana,*

and so begins
the verbal fevers
of my love-smitten Tourettes,
speaking in tongues
wild with metaphor,
swinging from branch to branch of simile,
rooting about for words
to match your roundness, your just succulency,
your sheer plump thighliness.

All morning I groom you with tiny lovenames.
I am a cat, you are my kitten, cowlicked
with locution. I am a sound nymph,
tickling you with alliteration, a Swedish masseuse,
rubbing you with vowels.
Who would have known my love
would rise up so fiercely, hover
delirious, in small bits of sound,
all day the adjectives landing and relanding,
determined to match your infinite perfection,
my sweet boy, my sweet boy.

## Field Work Post Partum, Huddled Above Them, She Thinks of South Sudan

High on the hill,
        she hovers over her sleeping children,
                20 below, winds howling,
                        snow stretched taut as cartilage.

Shadows stalk and billow,
        TV barks at the walls like a forgotten dog.
                Little wars slide
                        under the skin of their sleep.

Her son whimpers as an image pushes by,
        small explosions flash across his face, then settle like dust.
                In the low light of dawn, his belt, a coiled snake,
                        her piggy bank, a bloated skull.

Moon rises, setting fire to her sleeping girl.
        Wild mind, twitching foot,
                fins and gills slice through as a nightmare slashes about.
                But always the resurrection:

the next morning, tender as the light is weak,
        down stumbles her boy, train-wreck hair,
                grinning shyly—he knows
                        how much she loves his morning descent.

And the girl,
        still filled with moon and shadow,
                blond veins coiled around her,
                        inching no farther than her perch on the stairs.

Day after day, they surface, immaculately safe,
        into the squawking cacophony of light.

Meanwhile the Nile's belly swells,
  the tents' loose jowls flapping
    from the night's blue slaughter,

mothers swallow whole gulps of rain and wind,
  inside their skulls
    haggard dreams floating in and out.

The war winces and squeals, muted and labored
  as the moan of whales
    beneath the heaviness of ocean.

## The Country of Your Garden

Despite everything,
    the land mines, skull trees, splayed carcasses of rusted jeeps,
there you are again,
    deep in the humid thighs of July,
propagating Eden, little by little,
    as you walk, regal and measured,
lip curled, hands clasped behind your back,
    through the hay-strewn paths between raised beds,
the blazing democracy of your garden flourishing beyond
    all expectation, orange flags crawling up its borders,
butterflies, deer, children, dogs, crows,
    all clamor to be inside its gates, with you,
your fingers combing threads of cosmos,
    scabiosa, marigold, hosta
rubbing the furry brown abdomens of echinacea,
    soft and eerie as fontanel.
Huge mopped puppets of sunflowers
    bob in the wind
as you mercilessly tear the juicy weeds
    from what they know is good and sweet,
smoothing the soil back again
    as if you are putting a child
back to sleep in a hurry.

I'm waiving from the window,
    but you can't see me. There's still time
for me to cross the border,
    slip under the fence
and lie beneath you
    flooded with your rough, blond, soiled hands.

Come, after all these years, prune me.

I promise I could still rise up to you
  like the sunflower, wild-haired, glad and naïve

but hurry, you know our children won't sleep
  for much longer, gummy lips pouting as they follow
the rugged terrain of a scary dream's plot,

and before the morning steam burns off
  in another humid, hilly country
too close to Sudan

another war is brewing,
  for now, the machetes silently glistening
like stones in the river,
  the toddlers waddling with their pumpkin bellies,
the farmers methodically
  turning their dried beds of resentment
over and over. This country you have tried so earnestly to understand,
  soon to be dug up again with the claws of war,
the wild blood beds of the harvest,
  the fetid human compost strewn everywhere.

Hurry.

# Acknowledgments

The author wishes to acknowledge with gratitude the following journals and their editors:

*The Best American Poetry 2008*: "Skull Trees, South Sudan";

*The Sun*: "The Adoration," "The Sweet Hereafter," "Mud," "Milk," "Indra's Net," "Beneath the Sky, the Longing," "Email Elegy";

*The Kenyon Review*: "Skull Trees, South Sudan";

*Harvard Divinity Bulletin*: "Before His Execution, God Looks Down on a Yoga Class," "Lady's-slipper, Red Eft";

*Harvard Review*: "From Heaven, Mother Theresa Looks Down on Daya Dan";

*Salmagundi*: "Borders," "Lord's Resistance Army," "Opening Day, Mukaya";

*Green Mountains Review*: "The Crow," "Yolk," "Young West Meets My East," "Bus Station, Kampala, Uganda";

*Deep Travel: Contemporary Poets Abroad*: "Lost Boy";

*Image: Art, Faith, Mystery*: "War Metaphysics for a Sudanese Girl," "Dinka Bible";

*Agenda*: "What to Give Her—A Confession," "Moths";

*Anthropology and Humanism*: "Lost Boy," "Lord's Resistance Army," "Field Work Post Partum, Huddled Above Them, She Thinks of South Sudan";

*Consequence: a literary magazine addressing the culture of war*: "Field Work Post Partum, Huddled Above Them, She Thinks of South Sudan," "Christmas Eve, Kampala Uganda";

*The Salon*: "Attiak Refugee Camp, Northern Uganda," "The Hunger Sutras";

*Teesta-Rangeet—A Sikkimese Literary Journal*: "Young West Meets My East," "The Unraveling Strangeness";

*The Hypertexts*: "Skull Trees, South Sudan," "Milk."

## About the Author

Adrie Kusserow is Professor of Cultural Anthropology at St. Michael's College in Vermont, where she teaches courses on refugees, social inequalities, anthropology of religion, and medical anthropology. She received her MTS in Comparative Religion from Harvard Divinity School and her PhD in Social Anthropology from Harvard University. Her current ethnographic research and humanitarian work are in Bhutan and South Sudan. Along with some of the Lost Boys of Sudan resettled in Vermont, she and her husband helped found Africa ELI (www.africaeli.org), a nonprofit organization helping refugee girls attend schools in South Sudan. Her first book of poems, *Hunting Down the Monk*, was also published by BOA Editions, Ltd. Her poems have been published in journals such as *The Kenyon Review, Harvard Review, Green Mountains Review, The Sun, Harvard Divinity Bulletin, Salmagundi, Anthropology and Humanism,* and anthologized in *The Best American Poetry 2008, Deep Travel: Contemporary Poets Abroad,* and *The Poet and the World.* She lives in Underhill Center, Vermont, with her husband, Robert Lair and two children, Ana and Willem.

# BOA Editions, Ltd. American Poets Continuum Series

# Colophon

*Refuge*, poems by Adrie Kusserow,
is set in Adobe Garamond Pro, a digital font designed in 1989
by Robert Slimbach (1956– ) based on the French Renaissance roman
types of Claude Garamond (ca. 1480–1561) and the italics of
Robert Granjon (1513–1589).

The publication of this book is made possible, in part,
by the special support of the following individuals:

Anonymous
Anne C. Coon & Craig J. Zicari
Suressa & Richard Forbes
Anne Germanacos
X. J. & Dorothy M. Kennedy
Katy Lederer
Boo Poulin,
*in honor of Sandi Henschel,*
*in honor of Susan Burke & Bill Leonardi*
Cindy W. Rogers
Steven O. Russell & Phyllis Rifkin-Russell